I'm Not Normal; I'm Original

Palmetto Publishing Group
Charleston, SC

I'm Not Normal; I'm Original
Copyright © 2019 by Amy Schneider
All rights reserved

No portion of this book may be reproduced, stored in a retrieval system, or transmitted in any form by any means electronic, mechanical, photocopy, recording, or other except for brief quotations in printed reviews, without prior permission of the author.

First Edition

Printed in the United States

ISBN-13: 978-1-64111-387-8
ISBN-10: 1-64111-387-1

I'm Not Normal; I'm Original

AMY SCHNEIDER

When I was twenty-one years old, I was married and expecting my second child when my world came crashing down around me. I had a tingling sensation on the tip of my index finger on my right hand. The tingling turned to numbness and spread up my arm. The numbness turned into paralysis in my hand. I lost the use of my hand. I went to the doctor; he had no idea what was wrong with me. I was pregnant, and no testing could be done that would not affect the baby. I eventually got the use of my hand back and gave birth to a healthy baby girl.

I went through several trips to the doctor and hospital. The doctor said the only thing he could think of was a brain tumor. I had a CT scan to see where the tumor was, how big it was, and how much time I had left. Before the results of the scan were in, I lost the sight in my left eye. I was diagnosed with optic neuritis (inflammation of the optic nerve). Then I was told it was either multiple sclerosis (MS) or amyotrophic lateral sclerosis (ALS). The doctor ordered an MRI of my brain to see which one it was. I had a three-year-old and a 10-month-old at the time. What was going to happen to me? How would I take care of my family? Even worse, would I be alive to take care of my family?

I started to write letters to be given to my children when they reached all of the milestones in their lives (sixteenth birthday, eighteenth birthday, high school graduation, prom, etc.). Finally I was diagnosed with MS, a debilitating disease that affects the central nervous system. I thought my life was over.

I knew I had to be strong. I didn't want anyone, including my family, to see how scared I was.

I'M NOT NORMAL; I'M ORIGINAL

I was afraid of not knowing what was going to happen in the future, not knowing what to expect. Was there treatment and if so, what did it involve? I was devastated by the thought of the challenges ahead. I remember thinking to myself, *Why is this happening to me now? This isn't fair.*

I started searching for as much information on MS that I could find. I was relieved to find out MS is not a fatal disease. There are two types of MS, relapsing remitting and chronic progressive. I have the milder type, relapsing remitting. In both cases, MS attacks the lining of the nerve, called *myelin*, which interrupts the messages from the brain to other parts of the body. I think of nerves like a wire. The metal inside is the nerve, and the plastic covering around it is the myelin. Due to the fact that MS is an autoimmune disease, it can become active at any time. Stress, overexertion, and fatigue can also cause an exacerbation of the symptoms, which are numbness, weakness, exhaustion, blindness, and paralysis. The symptoms can last anywhere from a six-week period to an indefinite period. Only about 20 percent of the people who have MS are wheelchair bound. At that point, I was not.

I started going to physical therapy to learn an exercise regimen. I exercised day and night, no matter how tired or weak I felt. I made up my mind that this disease wasn't going to take control of my body and my life. I thought I knew everything there was to know about MS.

About a year later, I found that I didn't know everything. Attacks were coming monthly, not yearly. I didn't think I could win the fight against MS. I fought so hard to win that I was overworked and exhausted. The more I fought, the weaker I got. Before I knew it, I felt like MS was making me a prisoner in my home and, worse, a prisoner in my own body. I was unable to do anything that involved walking farther than a few feet. My doctor recommended using a wheelchair. I didn't want to think about using a wheelchair; I thought it was giving in to MS. I didn't want to admit that it had won.

In what I thought was a moment of weakness, I used the wheelchair. It was a cold, rainy day in early December. I wasn't feeling well, and walking was difficult. Christmas was coming soon; there was a lot of shopping to be done. My first stop was Toys "R" Us. The first thing I noticed was all of the boxes and toys on the floor in the aisles. It was difficult for me and my wheelchair to get around them. The store was very crowded; I was not able to get around all the shoppers to see what I wanted to look at.

At first, I felt ashamed. I had let MS win. But I was wrong. I realized the wheelchair was my friend, not my enemy. With the wheelchair, I was going out and doing things with my family instead of staying behind and being left out.

I didn't feel like a prisoner anymore, as I was able to get out and start to enjoy life. I realized I hadn't been handling MS as well as I had previously thought. I started to see MS as a constant companion, not an enemy. It goes everywhere I go. I am now able to do anything I want to do, including bowling and camping. I even learned to drive using hand controls.

I now understand that I can do anything as long as I realize I have limits on how much my body can take. I often make deals with my "companion." If it lets me do something that will push my body to the limit, I will make sure I get as much rest as my body needs to recover and regain my strength. Now that I understand MS and my limitations better, I can live a relatively normal life.

When I first found out that I had MS, I was devastated and an emotional wreck. I saw a wheelchair as a sign of weakness or even a threat that I was not a complete person. I now know that MS is not a death sentence. I have learned a lot about myself since I was diagnosed. I have often been asked if I regretted the pregnancy since the symptoms started while I was pregnant. I would rather have MS and my daughter, Heather, than no MS and no Heather. I have a lot more willpower and strength than I thought. There's a lot of truth to the saying "Knowledge is power." Now that I understand MS better and how my body responds to activities, I don't let MS run my life.

When people see a person in a wheelchair, they tend to feel sorry for them or think of them as helpless. I hope education will change this. I know I'm not "normal." I'm original. I don't feel sorry for myself, nor do I want people to feel sorry for me. The way I look at it, it could be worse.

It was the early eighties—I'm not sure what year. I was a normal thirteen-year-old when my parents got a divorce. As a child, I was closer to my father than my mother. He would play cards or board games with me, and get down on the floor and play with toys. He was "fun guy" while my mother did all the cooking, all the cleaning, and all of the discipline. As I got older, I could tell him anything, with no judgment. He knew when I started smoking cigarettes and partying. I told him about the first time I used marijuana, and marijuana laced with opium. I told him all about the parties and how drunk and high I was. He let me smoke cigarettes in front of him. He said he wanted to see me smoke, as if he got some kind of strange pleasure from watching me. I thought of him as "the cool parent." I thought we had a good relationship because I could tell him anything. Looking back, it was a boost to his ego and an opportunity to earn "brownie points" to allow me to have my way, although he had no concern for the possible affects it could have on my present and future health.

He remarried immediately after the divorce. The woman he married had two kids who were much older than me. In my opinion, both of her kids had issues of their own. They were very sheltered when they were children. For example, they both had to be home and inside when the streetlights came on when they were in high school. My stepmother said I had a "liberal childhood" and my mother was not "a good mother to me." When I was in high school, I had to be home at ten o'clock on weekdays and midnight on weekends; she considered that liberal.

I don't know why she thought my mother was not a good mother to me. My mother raised me to be very independent. She said she didn't want me "hanging from her apron strings." She wanted me to think for myself and make my own decisions. She didn't know I started smoking cigarettes, and she didn't know I was partying like I was. My mother was a great mother; she was the one who instilled in me morals, values, and a drive to improve myself. She disciplined me when I screwed up and took care of me when I was sick. She was a great role model, and she is a big part of the reason that I am who I am today.

My father found himself a "new family" to replace the "old family." My stepbrother was married and had a child, and my stepsister worked at Wendy's. Both lived at home with their mother. Sundays were spent at my father's house. I felt like an outsider when I was there, like I did not belong. Every Sunday, a local nightclub (the VIP) had under-twenty-one night. Admission was five dollars. My mom usually gave me the money to get in, but one week she told me to ask my father for the money. When I asked him, he said he would discuss it with my stepmom. It was only five dollars. I didn't see the need for a discussion. A little while later, he told me they had discussed it, and no, I could not have five dollars. They thought I should stay home and spend some time with "the family." I wasn't sure what that meant. First of all, I didn't consider them my "family," and second, the only thing we did together was eat dinner. My father and my stepmother would hang out in their bedroom, with the door shut.

They were big on hugs and kisses goodbye. I was getting ready to go home for the night and had to give Mark (my stepbrother) a hug and kiss good-bye. I was fifteen years old, and Mark was thirty. I thought he was kind of gross, and he smelled. I thought he was a pig, and I tried to keep my distance from him. This wasn't the first time he tried to cram his tongue down my throat. It *was* the first time he pushed me up against the wall, crammed his tongue down my throat, and tried to put his hand up my shirt.

When I grabbed his arm to push it away from me, he fought me and really pushed to try to get up my shirt. I pushed him away and ran away from him. This was spending time with "family?" Really?

The following Sunday when I was at my father's house, I told him what had happened. I thought he would protect me from Mark. He said he would talk to my stepmother about it and then said, "You're going to get high tonight, right?"

I said, "No, not tonight," and he asked why. I said it was because my friends and I didn't have any money. He asked how much it would cost. I said that twenty dollars would probably be enough. He gave me twenty dollars. Five dollars to get into the VIP needed a discussion, but twenty dollars to get high (and forget all about it) needed no discussion.

Even after I told my father what Mark did, he still told me to give him a hug and kiss good-bye, so I started saying I gave him a hug and kiss when I really didn't. When I was in my thirties, I realized that I should have told my mom. She would have protected me. But that would have meant breaking up the "family." I didn't want to be the one responsible for causing that. I wanted out of the façade that they called "family." I was always pushed into situations that included my stepbrother, even after I told my father what happened. To this day, I can still feel the muscle flexing in Mark's arm when I tried to push him away. I started refusing to do anything that involved Mark.

When I was seventeen and a senior in high school, a friend who had joined the military and moved away called to say hi and see how I was. His name was Harold, and he was in the Air Force and stationed in New Mexico. We kept in touch through letters and phone calls. We spent countless hours on the phone. We didn't talk about anything, just how the weather was in

Pittsburgh, how the weather was in New Mexico, what we had done that day, and what we were going to do the next day. In May 1986 Harold drove back to Pittsburgh on leave. He took me to my senior prom, and when he proposed, I immediately said yes. When I told my mother, she said, "If you are asking for my permission, you don't need it. You're eighteen and I can't stop you. But if you're looking for my blessing, you don't have it." I thought I was in love with him. Looking back on it, I realize I was not in love with him. I think I loved him, but was not in love with him. Getting married and moving to the other side of the country was just what I needed. Three days after my eighteenth birthday I left Pittsburgh with Harold, headed for New Mexico. It was the only way I could see to get away from Mark. My father encouraged me to get married. He didn't protect me from the evils that lurked in the world—he sent me running to them!

I was in an abusive marriage for seventeen years. I was emotionally as well as physically abused. Harold and I got married in New Mexico and were there for about two years; then he was stationed in England, we were there for three years and then in Texas for a year. For the first six years of marriage, I was in a different state and in a different country. Harold was all I had.

Harold was discharged from the Air Force in 1992, and we came back to Pittsburgh. I was not allowed to attend support groups. I was not allowed to go to any kind of counseling alone. Harold would not allow any supportive or government agency in the house. The windows had miniblinds and dark curtains that were pinned shut. He did not want anyone to see inside, as they would see what was going on. I was not allowed to go to the doctor unless he was there. He repeatedly called ACCESS (a door-to-door shared ride service for the handicapped and the elderly) and canceled my trips. I couldn't go anywhere, or if I did, when he found out through ACCESS where I was, he would find me, yell at me and take me home. I was kept from family and friends. I was completely isolated.

I used to ask the doctor to keep me in the hospital longer so I wouldn't have to go home. My legs were so stiff (a symptom of MS), and I was getting painful muscle spasms. It was difficult to walk. I was taking the maximum dose of muscle relaxers allowed. My doctor recommended a pump implanted in my abdomen that had a tube that went around my side and into my spinal cord. It would put the baclofen, a muscle relaxer, directly onto my spinal cord. Since it was put directly onto my spinal cord, the drug wasn't in my bloodstream, so I didn't get the side effects of extreme fatigue, and it was more effective. I was excited about the surgery. No more fatigue (I felt like a zombie), and maybe my legs would feel better.

I was excited about getting the pump, but Harold was pissed. He thought I should have consulted with him about the pump. He said it was selfish to make that decision without including him. I asked him why he should have anything to say about the pump; it was happening to my body. He said because it affected him and the kids also. I would have to be in the hospital to have the surgery. He had to work—who would take care of the kids? I thought, *Yeah, and there won't be anybody there to clean up after your ass.*

I had the surgery. It was the first time I stood up to him and did what I wanted anyway. Once the pump was in and working, I felt better. I had fewer spasms, and I didn't feel like a zombie. The downside to the surgery: the baclofen made my legs so weak that I couldn't walk. But if you ask me, it was worth it. I didn't feel like a zombie anymore, and the painful spasms were almost gone. I think walking is overrated. I can do just about anything in a wheelchair that you can do with your legs.

Harold started treating me like I was stupid. The stigma of using a wheelchair is since my legs don't work, my brain must not work either. I wasn't allowed to open any mail. I wasn't allowed to have access to money. When I started to complain about that, he opened a second checking account that was considered mine and deposited twenty dollars once a month. That way, I would have access to money. We had a car that had hand controls so he didn't have to take me everywhere, but he sold it because he said it gave me too much freedom.

I got a job that had direct deposit, and I had my paychecks deposited into my account. Harold was livid when he found out. I agreed to pay some of the bills out of my account, which calmed him down a little. Dinner had to be on the table and still hot when he got home, even though he never got home at the same time every day. If it wasn't, I had to be prepared for a long and loud lecture.

If he called and I did not answer, he would repeatedly call until I answered. When I finally answered the phone, he was pissed because I didn't answer the phone right away. Then he would yell at me and want to know why it took so long to answer the phone. He had a fit any time he couldn't find me or talk to me when he wanted to. One time, I was visiting a friend down the street. I didn't answer his repeated phone calls. He thought I fell down the steps or something and was lying in a pool of blood. He called the kids' school and told them not to let the kids get on the bus because he would pick them up and bring them home. I got home before the kids would have gotten home had they taken the bus. He was there and furious. He said that when I did not answer the phone, he'd assumed I'd fallen down the steps and was lying in a pool of blood. He didn't want the kids to come home and find me like that, so he had raced home before he was to pick the kids up. I got a real car beating for that.

It was March 7, 2002, an ordinary day: go to work, come home, make dinner, talk about the day with the kids, and off to bed. As usual, I couldn't get to sleep. Harold wasn't home yet, and I couldn't help wondering what was going to happen. Who was going to get it tonight? (Harold was abusive to the kids also.) What had I done wrong today? It was about 2:00 a.m.; I hear a car door slam shut, footsteps stomping up the metal ramp to the front door, the key going into the door, the door opening and slamming shut, the pounding of footsteps up the stairs to the bedroom. I thought, *Oh no, this doesn't sound good*. The light was turned on in my room, the briefcase was thrown to the floor, and the television was turned on. He didn't care if he woke me up. He took his clothes off and got into bed; he stank of beer and bourbon.

I pushed him away and said, "I don't want to." As usual, he didn't take no for an answer. I tried again: "I said no." It still didn't work. He just kept going. I felt his hands all over me, and he was going to climb on top of me and have his way. At that point, I was not there. I was somewhere else. I'd learned that if I thought I was somewhere else, it didn't happen, at least in my mind. That usually worked. When I didn't feel his weight on me, I'd know it was over. This time, it was working—until I felt the excruciating pain of his fist being rammed into my vagina. I screamed, "Ouch!"

He rolled over and went to sleep. Thank God, it was over, or so I thought. A couple hours later, he went to the bathroom and came back into the bedroom yelling, "You bitch, your damn period started."

I sat up to find myself lying in a large pool of blood, throbbing pain between my legs. I had been bleeding like that for a couple of hours. He looked to see where the blood was coming from. He said it was bad and I might need stitches. He said he didn't want to take me to the emergency room because they would say he raped me. *Well, you did rape me.* He said I would have to find some other way to get this taken care of.

I called the National MS Society and talked to Anne. I knew they had a nurse practitioner who would do a pap smear at home for people with MS. Anne thought I should go to the emergency room, so I called my PCP; he said I should go to the emergency room. This wasn't my fault. I couldn't move my legs, and I couldn't physically fight him off. He was a man; he didn't take no for an answer. He thought of himself as a superior to everything and everyone. No woman was going to tell him no. He did what he wanted when he wanted—nothing would stop him, especially someone as stupid as I was.

Harold said he would take me to the emergency room on his way to work if the bleeding didn't stop. We got to the emergency room at around 3:35 p.m. While we waited for the doctor, Harold told me it was all my fault that we were there. How was it my fault? I didn't ask to have MS. I didn't ask to have the movement in my legs taken away. I didn't ask him to rape me. And I sure as hell didn't ask to have my body mutilated by him against my will. He said, "If you would've let me put it up your ass, we wouldn't be here."

Nobody wanted to talk to me without Harold in the room. The doctor asked me if it was consensual, right in front of him. I felt like no one believed me. I said, "Yeah, right," and that was the end of it. Harold left shortly after that; he had to stop at home to clean up the blood that was all over the walls and carpet before he went to work.

The doctor I saw in the emergency room said it would have to heal on its own; too much time had passed since the tear happened. He said it wasn't worth doing surgery. I would have to self-cath to avoid incontinence. How was I to do that when I was completely mutilated? I went to another doctor for a second opinion. I wanted to know if it was as bad as I thought it was and if it could be fixed.

She said, "Yes, it's bad, and yes, it can be fixed. I'm calling the media team; I want that bastard."

I wound up having reconstructive surgery for a three-centimeter labial tear. The tear had to heal and be retorn, scar tissue had to be cut away, and the labia was reattached. Pictures were taken in the operating room to document the tear.

I separated from Harold and thought I was starting a new life of my own. He moved out and got an apartment. I thought life was good. I could open the mail now. One day I opened a credit card bill with over $1,200 in cash advances in a two-week period in a part of town that is well-known for having strip clubs and hookers. When I asked Harold what all the cash advances were for, he said he'd used it to buy groceries. I never saw $1,200 worth of groceries. There was food and pop in the refrigerator, but no one was allowed to eat or drink it. It was for him to take to work.

I filed for divorce and got a protection from abuse order (PFA). One night I woke up at 1:00 a.m. to find Harold standing over my bed looking at me. I'd thought having a PFA would keep him out of my house. The landlord said if they changed the locks, they would have to give him a key because he was on the lease. Harold repeatedly called me at all hours and came to my house when I wasn't home. He went through my mail. My mom sent me a birthday card that said, "Your very own mail." I put it with some other mail on my nightstand. A couple of weeks later, Harold asked me what my mom's comment meant. He would only know that if he'd seen the card. He was coming in and going through my stuff. I lived in a constant state of fear both before and after he moved out.

His defense to everything was that I had MS and it made me "mentally ill." He even went so far as to call my attorney to discuss my "mental issues." He said I did everything to myself: I raped myself, mutilated myself, and tortured myself. He used to say, "I'm sorry you got injured, but I didn't rape you. You never said no, you only said ouch." I made sure a copy of the PFA was on file at my local police department. I told them what was happening and explained that I was completely defenseless against Harold. I shouldn't have had to explain this! Look at me: I needed a wheelchair to get around. It should have been obvious that I physically couldn't run away and get help. My only defense was repeatedly calling the police. Harold would show up or call threatening to come over, and they said they would write a report. When I said that was not what it said on the PFA—it said if he violated it, he would be arrested—they said I would have to go to night court to get a warrant for his arrest. I explained my situation. How would I get there? I couldn't drive or take a bus, and I had to schedule ACCESS one day in advance. What about the PFA? What if he showed up or came into the house?

One time, an officer came to the house when Harold was in the yard screaming into the window. He told the officer that he was talking to the cat, not me. The officer said he was allowed to talk to the cat and left. After that event, I got copies of all the police reports filed for PFA violations and went to the district magistrate. He said he wouldn't give me a warrant because "Men don't like to be told what to do. If I give you this warrant, he might kill you. He is just tormenting you, and that isn't as bad as killing you." I showed him the pictures taken in the OR at the time of my surgery and asked if he could guarantee that it wouldn't happen again. He gave me a warrant but recommended that I not use it.

There was another PFA hearing after I got the warrant for Harold's arrest. His attorney walked in, went straight to my attorney, and said, "We're not leaving here with a PFA." My attorney showed him the pictures as proof to continue the PFA. His attorney said, "Could have been self-inflicted." What!? Why in the world would I do that to myself? I had limited use of my legs. It was physically impossible for me to do that to myself. I was stunned by his reaction.

The next step was to go in front of a judge who would hear both sides and make a decision to keep the PFA or let it expire. The two attorneys went to the judge's secretary to make an appointment. My attorney gave her the pictures that were taken in the OR and the arrest warrant. She asked his attorney if he was sure he wanted to do this. She remembered me from the first complaint, and she had an arrest warrant for his client. There was a police officer in the hall who would arrest his client. He was going to jail today. His attorney said, "OK, twelve-month PFA, your terms if you vacate the warrant." I thought about it for a minute. As much as I wanted Harold to go to jail, I didn't want my children to think of me as the person who'd had their dad arrested and put in jail. So I vacated the warrant and got a twelve-month PFA.

I spoke to a detective about filing rape charges, and he spoke to the district attorney about the case. I gave him the pictures, the OR report, and a letter from the doctor stating what the injury was and how it had been done. The doctor said she would testify to the fact that it was impossible for me to inflict that kind of injury on myself. The district attorney would not take the case, as it would be too hard to prove. First of all, he was my husband; a husband is allowed to have sex with his wife. Second, I had MS; my "mental issues" would be a problem.

On March 1, 2003, I couldn't take it anymore. I couldn't sleep, I couldn't eat, I constantly heard footsteps to my front door and the door opening. I couldn't breathe; it felt like my heart was going to pound out of my chest. I started to binge and purge. I was going to take some kind of control over my life. That was the only thing I could control. I received letters from Harold's attorney telling me that if I didn't quit talking about a rape that never happened, he would have me back in court. What?! He did rape me! He did mutilate me! I was scarred for life, and I had to live with that. Well, guess what? I couldn't live with that. This had to stop. The threats, the phone calls, the fighting, the pain, it had to stop. One of us had to die. If I killed him (that would be my preference), then I would go to jail for murdering an "innocent" man. My children would have no parents, and they would hate me for killing their father. And I would still live in torment.

The only way out was for me to die. I told everyone to get out of my house, leave me alone, and let me die. I had a handful of pills and decided this was it. Harold's girlfriend was picking the kids up. The kids told her , that I said to "let me die" and she called the police. I didn't know the police were there until an officer walked around the corner. I had been yelling at everyone to get the fuck out of my house. I knew the officer from all the times I'd called the police when Harold violated the PFA.

He said, "Now, Amy, you know I can't do that."

I said, "It's simple. You put one foot in front of the other, and soon you'll be walking out the door." I wound up going to the hospital to "be evaluated." I was admitted to the psych ward for about a week after I was assured that no one would find me. If Harold knew where I was, he would continue to torment me.

I was diagnosed with post-traumatic stress disorder (PTSD), obsessive-compulsive disorder (OCD), panic/anxiety, and depression. I couldn't understand. Why wouldn't they just let me die? This would be all over, and everybody would be happy.

Harold sued for custody of our two children and used my disability and "mental illness" as grounds. He turned my children against me. He somehow got a counselor to break into my medical record and find out what hospital I was in. He found me even after I'd been assured that my record was confidential. My children called me at the nurses' station and told me they didn't want to live with me anymore. They wanted to live with their dad. I didn't have any fight left. I gave up. In time, the kids would see what a creep he really was and come back.

Next, Harold sued me for child support. We met with a domestic relations officer. They took into account my income and his income and came up with an amount for child support. I would have to pay him $250 each month. But he was still in arrears from his child support when I had custody of the kids, so in the end, he had to pay me $250 per month. The divorce was absolutely ridiculous. It felt like I lived at the county courthouse.

In September 2006, I testified at a hearing in support of the Adult Protective Services Act (APS) (HB 2269) before the House Aging and Older Adult Services Committee of the Pennsylvania House of Representatives. This legislation would provide for protection of abused, neglected, exploited, or abandoned adults, including adults between the ages of eighteen and fifty-nine, who could not protect themselves from abuse due to a disability. I was nervous and terrified. My stomach was turning, I was nauseated, and I couldn't breathe. I was afraid of the usual questions people asked and things they said: "Why didn't you just leave him?" "You should've fought back." Victims in my situation are often judged. My reaction: walk a mile in my shoes before you judge me.

My testimony was successful. Two of the representatives commented and thanked me for telling my story. One of them even said that my testimony raised this issue in his mind. APS passed and took effect on April 7, 2011.

Time has passed, and I've had a lot of time to think. After I got away from Harold, my ex-husband, I realized that all the things he said about me were wrong. He said I was too stupid to be anything but a housewife. He said it was my fault that I couldn't walk. He said I'd let MS affect me and take the use of my legs and that I should be thankful that he didn't leave me when I was diagnosed. I will not let him and others like him destroy me. I've come too far to let anyone treat me the way he treated me.

Domestic violence is a serious issue in our society. Hopefully, education and awareness will change this. Many women have been killed in this country by an intimate partner. Many of them had PFAs. I understand that a piece of paper won't stop a bullet, but the more people that are aware there is a problem, the more people will be looking out for the signs of abuse.

The Constitution gives all Americans the right to life, liberty, and the pursuit of happiness. An abuser will take these rights before you even know it. It is my hope that writing this will raise awareness. Don't let what happened to me happen to anybody else.

Made in United States
North Haven, CT
05 April 2024